101 Things I Learned in Fashion School

101 Things I Learned™ in Fashion School

Alfredo Cabrera with Matthew Frederick

illustrations by Matthew Frederick
additional illustrations by Taylor Forrest

Matthew Frederick is the series creator, editor, and illustrator.

Grand Central Publishing
Hachette Book Group
237 Park Avenue
New York, NY 10017
www.HachetteBookGroup.com

Printed in Malaysia

First Edition: May 2010
10 9 8 7 6 5 4 3 2 1

Grand Central Publishing is a division of Hachette Book Group, Inc. The Grand Central Publishing name and logo is a trademark of Hachette Book Group, Inc.

Library of Congress Cataloging-in-Publication Data
Cabrera, Alfredo.
    101 things I learned in fashion school / by Alfredo Cabrera with Matthew Frederick.
        p. cm.
    ISBN 978-0-446-55029-1
    1. Clothing and dress—Study and teaching.   2. Fashion design—Study and teaching.   I. Frederick, Matthew.   II. Title.   III. Title: One hundred and one things I learned in fashion school.
    TT508.C32 2010
    746.9'2—dc22

                                                                                2009037649

Author's Note

A good fashion design curriculum encourages students to come up with informed, creative solutions to the problem of dressing people for their lives. In my years of teaching, I have found that the greatest obstacle to this goal is not the acquiring of technical proficiency or adequate intellectual information—certainly, with the availability of information today, the average eight-year-old is likely more sophisticated and fashion-savvy than ever—but in accepting the need to design for real people.

The perception on the part of many students (and sometimes instructors) is that reality—real customers with real needs—is the enemy of creativity. Real experience, it is feared, means drudgery, compromise, and mediocrity. The result is that most curricula tend toward the theoretical, with practical application addressed only to the extent it is considered unavoidable. It often seems that student designs more often resemble ideas than clothing.

It took me years as a working designer to *realize* the importance of identifying a real living customer and recognizing what he or she will and won't wear. Far from being anti-creative, it was for me the beginning of true creativity. For what is creativity if it isn't to take something existing in one's head and give it relevance in the real world?

The central purpose of this book, then, isn't to impart technical proficiency (although we hopefully will do some of that) or to challenge students creatively (though I hope we will do that too), but to give students some ways to connect the two. We hope to provide students with small reminders, touchstones, and catalysts to help them solve real problems creatively—and creative problems realistically.

I hope that students and designers will keep this little book handy while researching, designing, swatching, and illustrating. I hope the history lessons help readers understand that innovation happens in context and through reaction to what came before; that the lessons in organization motivate the development of a holistic design process; that the lessons in illustration demonstrate the importance of communication; and that the business lessons lend a sense of the designer's role in the larger world.

Alfredo Cabrera

Acknowledgments

From Alfredo

Thanks to Karin Yngvesdotter, Michele Wesen-Bryant, Howard Davis, Joseph Sullivan, and Evelyn Lontok-Capistrano for their help, guidance, advice, and support.

From Matt

Thanks to Karen Andrews, David Blaisdell, Sorche Fairbank, Taylor Forrest, Sarah Handler, Tracy Martin, Camille O'Garro, Karyn Polewaczyk, Janet Reid, Kallie Shimek, Flag Tonuzi, Tom Whatley, and Rick Wolff.

101 Things I Learned in Fashion School

Fashion was born in the 12th century.

There are two ways to clothe the human form. In **draping**, simple pieces of cloth are wrapped around the body, with the excess falling in natural folds. This was the earliest method of making clothing from textiles. However, while draped clothing was traditionally ephemeral—it lost its shape when not in contact with the body—draped clothing today usually has a tailored understructure.

Tailoring dates to the Early European Renaissance of the 12th century, when a celebration of the natural world in science, philosophy, and art brought about a focus on the human form. The draped robe was divided into multiple pieces to more closely fit the body. These pieces evolved into *patterns* that were used to create multiple garments. The advent of tailoring was thus the birth of fashion.

Fashion designers create collections, not simply individual garments.

Depending on the size of a design house, a collection may have anywhere from 12 to 400 garments. A designer plans a collection so that every item complements the others; they can be worn together or individually.

A designer gives attention to every piece in a collection, including underpinnings and layering pieces, not just the exciting gowns, suits, dresses, and other major items. After you've worked hard to cultivate a customer for the primary garments, why send him or her elsewhere for the rest of the outfit?

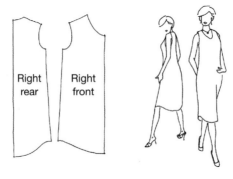

Pattern (def. 1) for a sleeveless dress

Fashion-ese

Collection: 1. a thematically cohesive group of garments created by a designer for a season. 2. a category of clothing, e.g., an outerwear or swimwear collection.

Drape: 1. the reaction of a fabric to gravity, how it "falls." 2. to manipulate a fabric on a dress form while creating a design.

Fabric story: a group of fabric samples conveying a designer's selections for a collection. Sometimes referred to as a fabric storyboard or a fabrication.

Finish: 1. the surface texture of a woven fabric. 2. a final fashion drawing.

Fit: 1. the way in which a garment drapes or falls on the body. 2. to make adjustments to a muslin or sample on a model or mannequin.

Line: 1. the general silhouette or flow of a garment, e.g., "the line of an evening gown." 2. a synonym for *collection*, e.g., "our fall line emphasizes a retro look."

Muslin: 1. an inexpensive, finely-woven cotton fabric. 2. a prototype garment, created to work out design and fit; called a muslin regardless of the fabric.

Pattern: 1. a template for the individual pieces of a garment. 2. a visual design, e.g., check, stripe, or floral.

Diane von Furstenberg's wrap dress

Fashion is born from ideas.

A single dress or t-shirt can be created without an underlying concept, but an entire collection cannot. A fashion collection must be driven by an idea that transcends material reality, and is based in an attitude toward or approach to life, art, beauty, society, politics, and self. Examples of popular idea-driven fashions include:

- **Diane von Furstenberg's wrap dress:** It was motivated and preceded by the broad-based entry of women into professional workplaces and a desire to project authority while remaining feminine and sexy.
- **Giorgio Armani's relaxed, elegant tailoring:** It responded to the emergence of new businesses and more informal business models in the 1970s and 1980s, ultimately paving the way for the now familiar "casual Fridays."
- **Grunge:** Before it became a popular fashion look, grunge was a movement that sought to reject lifestyle-consciousness.

"Fashion is the attempt to realize
art in living forms."

—SIR FRANCIS BACON (paraphrase)

1   2   3   4   5

The Five C's of good pre-design

The fashion design process is complex and iterative, and does not proceed in exactly the same way for all designers. Nonetheless, a progression of consistent pre-design steps is identifiable in the processes of successful fashion designers:

1 **Customer:** Understand who you are designing for.

2 **Climate:** Know the season of the year for which the collection is intended.

3 **Concept:** Explore and create a "big idea" that will inspire the entire collection.

4 **Color:** Determine a suitable color palette.

5 **Cloth:** Investigate and identify the fabrics for the garments in the collection.

The design of individual garments proceeds in earnest only *after* arriving at the cloth.

Know who you *aren't* designing for.

A fashion designer must know much about the intended customer: How old is he or she? Where does he live? How does she make a living? How much does she earn? Where does he shop? What does she already wear? What is she not being offered? To what goals does he or she aspire? Such questions help a designer frame an intuitive box around a fashion design problem.

When a customer is particularly difficult to define, it can be helpful to define an entirely different customer—one for whom the product is absolutely *not* intended. The effort involved in assessing the lifestyle needs of another usually helps a designer better grasp the intended customer.

Design outside in, top to bottom, big to small.

The many items comprising a collection—suits, skirts, slacks, jackets, blouses, sweaters, accessories, and more—have to be carefully coordinated. Yet it is impossible to conceive and design everything at once. How does one prioritize?

Design outside in: The design of outer garments such as coats and jackets should be undertaken before the garments they partially conceal, such as vests, blouses, and underpinnings.

Design top to bottom: Garments near the face are inherently more important than and should receive design priority over clothing worn lower on the body.

Design big to small: Large pieces of clothing such as dresses, suits, and coats should almost always be designed before shirts, blouses, vests, and knit tops.

These three strategies roughly correlate with the apportionment of the fashion dollar: Customers tend to spend more on items worn outside other items, on items closer to the face, and on larger items.

Create an organized fabric story.

Coat/outerwear weights: heavy weight fabrics for fall/winter, as well as medium weight technical fabrics and fabrics that have been treated for water repellence for spring/summer.

Jacket or bottom weights: medium weight fabrics for structured garments including suits, pants, skirts, tailored dresses, and jackets not worn as outerwear.

Dress/blouse weights: light weight, sheer, and silky fabrics for shirts, blouses, flowing dresses, skirts, gowns, and other soft garments.

Sweater weights: bulky, warm yarns for fall/winter as well as fine, cool yarns for spring/summer.

Cut & sew knits: for underpinnings, casual dresses or gowns.

Novelty fabrics: have a feature that makes them ideal for special items but limited for basic use, such as lace, leather, fur, PVC/vinyl, etc.

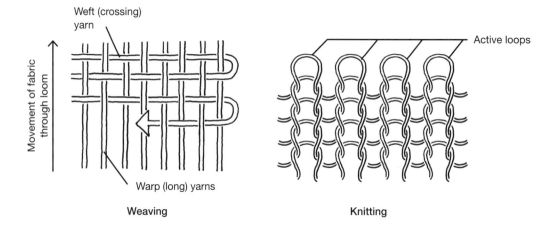

Weft (crossing) yarn

Movement of fabric through loom

Warp (long) yarns

Weaving

Active loops

Knitting

Weaving and knitting

Most fabrics are made by weaving or knitting. **Woven fabrics** are made by interlacing a continuous yarn repeatedly through a series of parallel yarns. The parallel yarns (*warp* yarns) are held in place by a *loom*, and the crossing yarn (*weft* yarn) is laced through them in an "over-under" manner. After each trip across, the weft yarn reverses direction.

Knitted fabrics are made from a single continuous yarn interlocked onto itself. A row of active loops (called *stitches*) is held in place by a needle as another series of loops is pulled through it with a second needle. This produces a new row of active stitches, and the process is repeated.

Netting, felt, and PVC (polyvinyl chloride) are neither woven nor knitted, and are of comparatively limited use in fashion design.

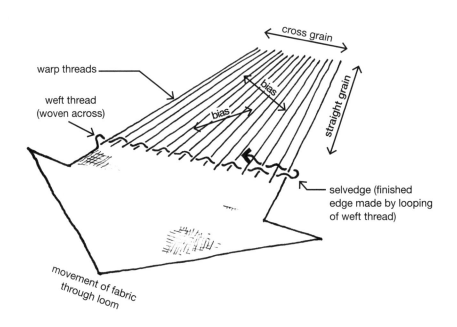

cross grain

warp threads

weft thread
(woven across)

bias

bias

straight grain

selvedge (finished
edge made by looping
of weft thread)

movement of fabric
through loom

Go with (or against) the grain.

Straight grain (or warp) is the long direction of woven fabric; it is the direction in which it moves through a loom. The straight grain is the strongest axis; it has almost no stretch or "give." Most garment pieces are cut "on the straight"; that is, with the straight grain running vertically (perpendicular to the floor) when the wearer is standing.

Cross grain (or weft) refers to the short direction of woven fabric, across the loom. Fabric usually has a little bit of stretch in the direction of the cross grain. When a jacket is cut on the straight, the cross grain allows it to feel a little stretchy when the wearer folds his or her arms.

Bias is the 45-degree angle between the straight and cross grains. Fabric has the most stretch in the bias direction. Before spandex, the only way to get significant stretch from woven fabric was to cut it on the bias—a practice which can be pro-hibitively expensive due to its considerable waste.

Design *into* the fabric.

Novice designers often select fabrics only after creating a garment's silhouette. But a well conceived garment can be destroyed by cutting it in the wrong cloth. Many fabrics simply will not do what a designer wants. Silk gazar, for example, is thin and paper stiff and will not accept close tailoring or free draping.

Before beginning the design of a garment, the fabric group for the collection must be considered in detail. Garments are designed *into* their fabrics, not the other way around.

Cotton plant

Cotton is a fiber, not a fabric.

13

A fiber is a filament of raw material, the smallest essential element of a garment. It may be very long or as short as a few centimeters. Fibers are made into thread or yarn by spinning, and are subsequently woven or knitted into cloth. Fiber types are categorized as follows:

Natural fibers are found in nature. The four basic natural fibers are silk, wool (animal fibers), cotton, and linen (vegetable fibers). Others include cashmere, alpaca, vicuna, ramie, and hemp, all of which can be costly and difficult to use compared to the basic fibers.

Manufactured fibers are created by processing natural cellulose—the same basic material as cotton and linen. Examples include rayon, acetate, and modal.

Synthetic fibers are created by forcing a liquid chemical through a small hole to produce a continuous strand or filament. Common synthetics are nylon, polyester, and acrylic.

 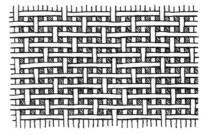

3/3 twill weave   Satin weave

Satin is a weave, not a fabric.

14

Fabric weaves are generally distinguishable by their surface, or face, characteristics. Innumerable faces are available; some common ones include:

Twill has raised diagonal lines on the face. Examples include denim, cavalry twill (a rugged, flexible fabric), and foulard (a silk fabric). Commonly used in military uniforms.

Satin is characterized by a shiny, smooth face. Examples include duchesse (a stiff, glossy silk), charmeuse (a shiny, watery fabric), and peau de soie (a silk with a dull luster.

Jacquard has a woven pattern visible on the face as a subtle change from shiny to matte. Examples include damask (a rich tonal-patterned fabric), brocade (a fabric with a multi-colored pattern), and matelassé (resembles quilting). Useful in both fashion and home decor.

Pile is characterized by a fuzzy or hairy surface called *nap*. Examples include velvet (a fine, short nap), terry cloth (a spongy, looped nap used for bath towels), and corduroy (a surface with parallel cords).

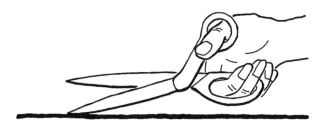

Always keep the bottom blade in full contact with the table.

How to cut fabric

15

1 Lay the fabric flat on a table; don't attempt to cut it while holding it in front of you. The table should be positioned to allow access to all sides.

2 Smooth out all creases and bubbles, using an iron as needed. Make sure the straight and cross grains are exactly perpendicular—something that requires particular care with many fabrics, such as chiffon and charmeuse.

3 Mark cut lines clearly, whether making a straight or curved cut. If using a pattern or template, pin it to the fabric.

4 Use very sharp shears. Never use shears that have been used to cut paper.

5 Grip the shears firmly, and cut smoothly along your lines or at the edge of the paper pattern. Stop each cutting stroke before the blades fully close to avoid a choppy edge. Continue each cut slightly beyond the desired stopping point.

6 To make a cut in a different direction, do not lift or move the fabric. Instead, walk around the table and cut from a natural, more convenient angle.

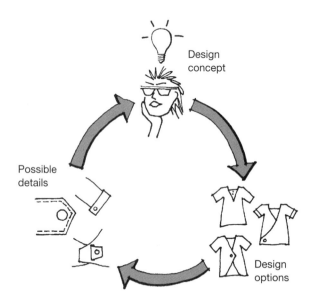

Design
concept

Possible
details

Design
options

16

Details aren't add-ons to a design concept; they're essential to *formulating* a design concept.

A successful design is conceptually driven, but a concept is rarely, if ever, understood without developing the details. Do blow-up drawings of garment details throughout your design process, even early on. Don't just explore decorative flourishes, but also highly functional considerations such as pockets, closures, and seams.

Sometimes details can back-drive the design process: A designer may create a garment with a specific silhouette in mind, but once detailed the silhouette may change dramatically. And occasionally, a great idea for a detail can become the inspiration for an entire collection.

If you don't know how the garment you've designed will be made, you haven't designed anything.

17

A good designer doesn't rely on more technically astute persons to turn his or her creations into workable realities. To the contrary, the more accomplished the designer, the more thoroughly he or she engages in technical execution—structure, seaming, hardware, patternmaking, fabric selection, and more. To do otherwise is, paradoxically, to *cede* control of the design process and put the "brilliant" designer at the *bottom* of the creative food chain. Indeed, as a design concept proceeds toward realization, patternmakers, sample-hands, models, and even salespersons will seek to change it to suit their needs. A savvy individual among them might dismiss the objections of a poorly informed designer by saying, "What you want can't be done." How would an uninformed designer know otherwise?

Angles can be
split and/or
rotated as long
as pivot point
and total dart
angle remain
constant.

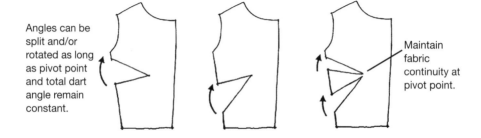

Maintain
fabric
continuity at
pivot point.

Three options for a bust dart

18

How to pivot a dart

A dart is a fold of fabric sewn in place, used to eliminate excess fabric and accommodate the three-dimensional curves of the body. A dart is distinct from a seam in that a seam joins two pieces of fabric while a dart provides localized adjustment to one piece of fabric. Darts are used much more frequently in women's clothing than men's.

A single dart can be divided into two or more smaller darts, pleats, tucks, gathers, etc., as long as their combined angles equal the total dart-control angle.

Conan O'Brien

19

Random hypothesis

Your shoes say who you are; your hair or hat says how you wish to be perceived.

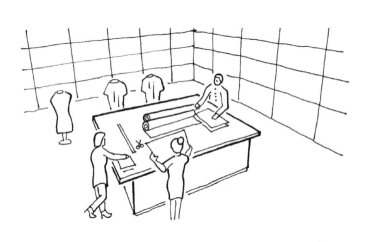

Who does what

Fashion designer: conceives, designs, and directs the creation of a fashion collection or fashion category.

Production manager: creates costing and logistical plans for a fashion house or design firm.

20

Patternmaker: determines the exact two-dimensional shapes of fabric needed to make a design realizable as a three-dimensional garment.

Cutter: cuts fabric in the shapes determined by the patternmaker; works in a fashion house or factory.

Sample-hand: constructs the first sample of a garment for the designer. Sample-hands include tailors, sewers, knitters, and embroiderers. Workers who fill two or more of these roles are called *sample-makers*.

Machine operator: a factory sewer (although never a sample-hand); in a past era, "seamstress" referred to a female machine operator.

Fashion editor: creates themes for photo shoots in the media and selects styles from various designers to illustrate those themes.

Buyer: an employee of a retail store or chain who selects the apparel it will sell.

21

The average adult is 7-1/2 heads tall.
A fashion figure is at least 9 heads tall.

A fashion illustration exists to represent and sell the *idea* behind a garment. Therefore, its design must appeal to the oft-held aspirations of the fashion customer: to be young, slender, elegant, graceful, and hip. The elongated figure tends to suggest all these things.

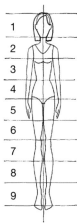

1

2

3

4

5

6

7

8

9

How to draw a 9-head-tall fashion figure

Draw a vertical line and mark ten ticks to create nine equal segments.

22

Segment 1: Draw an egg or ellipse for the head.

Segment 2: In the middle of the segment, draw the shoulders sloping down-ward. Total width is about 2½ times the width of the head.

Segment 3: Locate the bustline in the upper third.

Segment 4: Draw the waist at the top of the segment, a little more than half the shoulder width. Align the elbows with the waist. Draw the hips at the bottom, about two heads wide.

Segment 5: Draw the crotch with a short horizontal line about ¼ of the way down. Align the wrists with the crotch and extend the hands to the bottom of the segment.

Segments 5–9: The legs and feet. The thighs start at the top of Segment 5, the knees are centered near the top of Segment 7, and the ankles are located in the upper third of Segment 9.

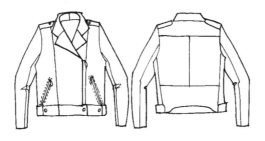

Front and rear flats of
a motorcycle jacket

Illustration types

A fashion designer must be a good communicator. Four primary drawing types are used to communicate design intentions:

23

Croquis (CROAK-ee): a quick working illustration that depicts the general silhouette, proportions, and look of a garment. Working out the design of a garment usually takes at least three croquis, and often many more. Most designers maintain a sketchbook for continual croquis-ing.

Blow-up: a magnified illustration of an area of a garment, used to convey details not visible in an overall view, such as construction, stitching, hardware, and embellishments.

Flat: a technical illustration showing a garment laid flat in exact proportion, used to communicate in detail its structure and functionality.

Finish: a fully rendered, final illustration of a fashion figure, usually 12 to 15 inches tall, communicating the attitude or sensibility of the garment or collection and the intended customer. Styling and accessories that are not necessarily part of the collection are often included.

Draped clothes are nearly impossible to sketch accurately.

24

The three-dimensional behavior of tailored clothing is fairly predictable and easy to portray in a two-dimensional sketch, but garments that use significant draping usually are not. Different fabrics drape in different ways, often producing a silhouette unlike the one intended. Patterned fabrics add further complexity, as crucial portions can disappear into folds and recesses.

When designing garments with significant draping, work directly with fabric as you sketch.

Complex garments: process usually starts here

Conventional garments: process usually starts here

How to turn a sketch into a garment prototype

25

Two methods are used to develop a design sketch into a three-dimensional garment. Complex garments are often created by first draping the muslin fabric over the form, then tucking, darting, and adjusting it to approximate the desired fit. The muslin is then removed and refined on the table to more accurately represent the pattern pieces.

Conventional garments are often created first on the table by adapting existing garment patterns. The patterns are then transferred to the muslin and refined on the dress form.

In both instances, multiple iterations are required to create a final muslin prototype. Once the prototype is set, it is fitted to a model, and after final adjustments, the garment is cut in the intended fabric.

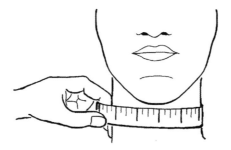

Take neck measurements loosely enough to
allow the comfortable insertion of a finger.

Take measurements with ease.

Measurements should not be taken tightly on the body or dress form, but with a slight ease in the measuring tape. Important measurements include:

26

Bust: Take around the apex of the bust and around the chest/under the arms. Don't follow the slope of the breasts; keep the tape horizontal all the way around.

Waist: Take around the smallest part of the torso.

Hip: Take approximately 7" below the waist, over the largest curve of the buttocks.

Other key measurements include center-front, center-back, shoulder, neck, cross-chest, cross-back, shoulder slope, and side seam.

Haute couture is protected by French law.

27

Only fashion companies judged by the Chambre de commerce et d'industrie de Paris (the Paris Ministry for Industry) as meeting specific qualifying criteria may use the label "haute couture," or "high dressmaking." A member of the Federation of Couture Houses must:

- design made-to-order clothing for private clients, with one or more fittings.
- keep an atelier (design studio) in Paris employing at least 15 people.
- present a collection of at least 35 looks for both day and evening wear to the French press twice each year.

be·spat·ter (be spat′ ər, bi-) *vt.* to spatter, as with soil or slander; sully

be·speak (be spēk′, -bi) *vt.* **-spoke** (-spōk), **-spo·ken** or **-spoke** , **-speak·ing** **1** to speak for in advance; reserve **2** to be indicative of; show. From O.E. *besprecan*, "to speak about"; 1580± "to speak for, to arrange beforehand, to ask for in advance"; 1600s—1700s, "custom-made, made to order"

best (best) *adj.* [[OE *betst*]] **1** *superl. of* GOOD **2** the most excellent, suitable, desirable, etc. **3** the largest portion *[*the *best* part of a year*] –adv.* **1** *superl. of* WELL **2** in the highest manner *–n.* **1** the highest or

28

Bespoke tailoring

Bespoke tailoring is true custom tailoring for men. It refers to suits and shirts made to the exact specifications of the wearer, from fabric to styling to fit. Originally, the term was not restricted to high quality garments, but today is the men's equivalent of haute couture: Use of both terms is legally guarded by the French government.

Sometimes

Always

Never

Buttoning of two- and three-button jackets

Rules for the traditional man's suit

Fabric: 100% wool or cotton; silk, synthetics, and blends are to be avoided. Traditional patterns such as herringbones, windowpanes, and tweeds should be executed in gray or brown wool; pinstripes and chalk stripes in gray, navy, or black wool. Cotton suits should be in light colors such as tan or white. Seersucker suits may be gray/white, navy/white, or red/white.

29

Jacket: Should fit the body comfortably but closely, with no wrinkles when buttoned. Shoulders should neither protrude nor be too narrow. The chest and lapels should lie flat. The collar lies flat against the back of the neck, with ½" of shirt collar visible. Jacket sleeves extend 1" past the wrist with shirt cuffs peeking out ½". Double breasted suits flatter those with broad chests, single breasted the slim. Fewer buttons elongate a short torso, although only a white dinner jacket should be one-button. One or two vents are acceptable; ventless jackets look inexpensive.

Trousers: Should be neither too roomy nor so snug that the front pockets flare open. Use pleats only with wool, and only one pleat per side. The crease should break in the front. Bottoms may be cuffed or uncuffed; the back should touch the shoe heel and the front should cover the shoe upper.

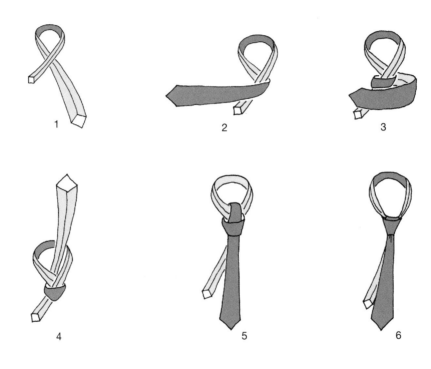

1   2   3
4   5   6

How to tie a Matt knot

The collar and tie

The width and spread of the shirt collar, the width of the jacket lapels, and the width and weight of the tie are interdependent design considerations. A suit with wide lapels should usually be worn with a spread-collar shirt and a full knot, such as a Windsor, for proportional consistency. A suit with narrow lapels should usually be paired with a narrow-spread collar and a small tie knot, such as a four-in-hand. The tip of the tie should always meet the belt buckle.

The most common necktie knots are:

Windsor: a classic, large, symmetrical formal knot.

Half-Windsor: a smaller, simpler version of the Windsor, suited to medium or wide collar spreads and ties of medium weight.

Four-in-Hand: a casual, slightly asymmetrical tie knot that leaves extra tie length. Works well with narrow collar spreads and on very tall men.

Pratt: a small to medium sized symmetrical knot that uses less tie length than the Windsor; starts with the reverse side facing forward.

Matt: a very narrow symmetrical knot, starts reverse side forward. Effective for showing off a tie with a very full drape.

"Clothes make the man. Naked people have little or no influence on society."

—MARK TWAIN

Fashion is a barometer of culture.

32

Fashion responds to culture, although the specific ways in which it does so are impossible to predict. When the 19th Amendment granted women the right to vote, women bobbed their hair and raised their hemlines above the knee. But during the Great Depression when conservatism might have been expected, fashions became glamorous in the extreme, as embodied by Golden Age of Hollywood actresses such as Marlene Dietrich, Ginger Rogers, and Jean Harlow. In the 1980s, when women first entered the professional ranks in large numbers, shoulder pads were introduced to create stronger physical presence. Men's fashions soon began featuring their own exaggerated shoulder pads.

Fashion designers must grasp broad cultural developments, but should design naturally rather than attempt to make overly literal fashion responses.

Garment designed by Yohji Yamamoto

Conceptual design began at Hiroshima.

33

What is known as conceptual design today is traceable to the atomic bombs dropped on Hiroshima and Nagasaki by the United States in World War II. Three Japanese designers—Rei Kawakubo, Issey Miyake, and Yohji Yamamoto—grew up in their wake and became the avant-garde of the late 1970s and early 1980s. Together they paved the way for the end of Western hegemony on fashion and profoundly altered prevailing notions of beauty.

Before rock and roll, young people dressed like their parents.

34

In the 1960s, the baby boom, the ascension of rock and roll as a cultural phenomenon, and widespread dissatisfaction in American and Western societies helped produce a turbulent, youth-centric counterculture. Up to this point, teens and children were usually perceived—and clothed—as younger or smaller versions of their parents.

Women's fashions change every day; men's change every few centuries.

35

In the West, men's and women's fashions changed with similar frequency before the modern era. When the Enlightenment proclaimed the equality of all men, the need for fashion to distinguish social rank was somewhat neutralized. Additionally, the standardization of military uniforms meant that men no longer went to war in their own clothes, further encouraging dress conformity. The tailored man's suit emerged as a great social leveler in the 19th century, and it has changed very little since.

The 20th century in women's fashion

Trend/Silhouette	Era/Influence	Important Designer
Hourglass	Art Nouveau	Charles Frederick Worth
No corset/hobble skirt	Asia/Suffrage	Paul Poiret
Boyish flattened curves	19th Amendment	Gabrielle "Coco" Chanel
Bias cuts	Hollywood	Madeleine Vionnet, Adrian
Broad shoulder/A-line skirt	WWII	Elsa Schiaparelli, Mainbocher
Pointed bust/full skirt	New Look	Christian Dior, Cristóbal Balenciaga
Babyish flattened curves	Youth culture	André Courrèges, Mary Quant
Rich hippies	Street clothes	Yves St. Laurent, Roy Halston
Broad shoulder/short skirt	Conspicuous consumption	Giorgio Armani, Christian Lacroix
Minimalism	Belgium/Grunge	Marc Jacobs, Helmut Lang

H-line

A-line

A fashion designer jump-started France's post-WWII economy.

After World War II, the French textile mills lay quiet due to manufacturing having been shifted to the war effort. Christian Dior helped restart the textile industry by designing unusually full skirts requiring many yards of cloth. Additionally, he presented radically different seasonal silhouettes that got women shopping and money flowing. But Dior's New Look would not have been embraced had it been a marketing strategy only; more significantly, it consciously reaffirmed the femininity sacrificed during the war.

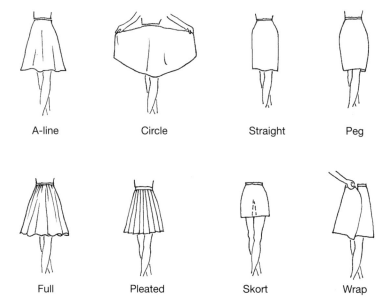

A-line   Circle   Straight   Peg

Full   Pleated   Skort   Wrap

Basic skirt types

A-line: has a slight overall flare, giving it the approximate shape of the letter 'A'.

Circle: made from a circle of fabric with a hole cut in the center for the waist. Very full at the bottom, fits the waist and hips without darts or pleats. A half-circle is a variant.

Full: a generously sized skirt adapted to the waist by gathers or pleats. Varieties include the dirndl, pouf, and bubble.

38

Peg: similar to a straight skirt, but the hem is smaller than the hips, so the skirt follows the contours of the body. A trumpet skirt adds a flare at the hem.

Pleated: a full skirt with multiple creased folds of fabric to create an accordion or bellows effect and to fit the waist and hips.

Skort: a hybrid of shorts and skirt, designed to resemble a skirt.

Straight: hangs straight from hips to hem, the measurements of both being equal. A yoke or darts are used to fit the waist and hips. Types include the pencil (mid-length) and hobble (a long skirt that prevents the wearer from walking with a normal stride).

Wrap: wraps around the body with an overlap and fastener. Types include the kilt (a pleated variant) and sarong.

"Free" accessories reduce the quality of a garment.

39

When belts, suspenders, scarves, jewelry, or other adornments are attached to a garment, their additional cost requires compensation. Consequently, such attachments are usually of low quality, cheapening what otherwise might have been an attractive item; or the garment itself will be of lower quality than its unadorned counterparts.

Designer beware: The impulse to include an accessory with a garment usually indicates a desire to use outside elements to validate a weak design.

Added value

Fashion customers often need to be convinced to buy a new garment that, in effect, they already own. How does a designer sell a basic sweater or skirt to a customer who doesn't really need it?

40

Added value (or value added) details can help reach the hesitant buyer, particularly in the middle, lower, and casual segments of the fashion market. Value added details are those that are inherently necessary to a garment but are executed in a novel or interesting way that doesn't add significantly to cost. Common examples include unique buttons, special stitching, interestingly shaped pockets, and contrasting or patterned linings.

You can't add value where some doesn't already exist.

41

It is better to aim too high—by overconceptualizing a garment or collection or by attempting design moves that are overly effusive—and have to "water it down," than to attempt to augment a middling design concept that lacks true inspiration.

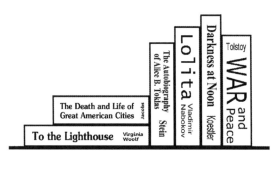

"The commonplace may be understood as a reduction of the exceptional, but the exceptional cannot be understood by magnifying the commonplace."

42

—EDGAR WIND (1900–1971)
"An Observation on Method" (paraphrase)

The dressmaker

Before Ready-to-Wear clothing, women either made their own clothes or had them made by dressmakers. Dressmakers differ from fashion designers in that they do not design wholly new fashions, but copy or adjust the fashions of the day. Often they add flourishes such as ruffles, flounces, covered buttons, spaghetti straps, and ribbon trims. Today, such highly feminized, applied details are still referred to as dressmaker details whether or not created by a dressmaker.

Dressmaker detailing is important in fashion design, although the term is sometimes used derogatorily to describe a garment in which the designer's attention was directed to flourishes and appliqué rather than more essential design considerations of silhouette, fit, line, and tailoring.

43

Give it a reason.

Even the most highly expressive fashions must answer to functional needs: structure, fit, use, even the method of manufacture. For this reason, aesthetic design moves should be viewed as opportunities to enhance purpose. When drawing exploratory lines while designing, immediately consider how they can make the garment fit or work better. A dramatic asymmetrical design move might become an opportunity to locate a pocket or hardware fastening. The introduction of color blocking might be used to draw attention to the structure of the garment. An uneven hem, intended to exalt the flow of a fabric, might help show off a contrasting lining or an interesting shoe or boot.

Design gestures justified only by "I like it" rarely turn out to be something a designer actually does like when the final garment is realized.

44

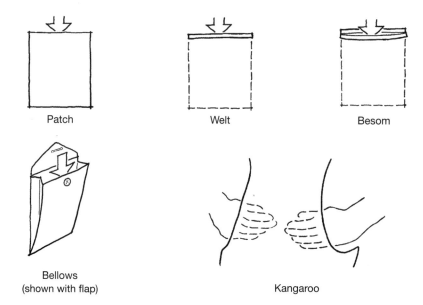

Patch

Welt

Besom

Bellows
(shown with flap)

Kangaroo

Patch pockets imply utility. Welt and besom pockets suggest refinement.

The most common pockets are:

Patch: a piece of fabric is stitched onto the outside of a garment on three sides, leaving the fourth side open. Patch pockets suggest functionality, in the manner of painter's or carpenter's pants and often do not look coherent on elegant garments.

Welt: a very common pocket type, made by slitting into the fabric of the garment and hiding the pocket bag inside.

Besom: a variation on the welt, made in the manner of a large buttonhole, with the two sides of the opening finished with piping or welts.

Bellows: a variation on the patch, constructed to extend away from the garment.

Kangaroo: an informal pouch-like pocket, usually open on two sides but sometimes at the top, located on the front of the torso.

Turn seams into style lines and style lines into seams.

Good designers strategically place and manipulate seams to maintain fit while creating interesting, innovative aesthetic effects. They work in the opposite direction, too—turning style lines into structurally useful elements. When a seam is introduced into a garment for aesthetic effect—perhaps to inset a contrasting fabric or emphasize the body's curves—turn it into an opportunity to better fit the garment to the body.

Simple clothes aren't simple to design.

When superfluous design elements are eliminated from a garment, more subtle considerations—proportion, line, fit—are magnified. This calls for a refined understanding of anatomy (e.g., how the neckline sits in relation to the clavicle), geometry, balance, positive and negative space, and the harmony of parts to whole.

47

	Height	Weight	BMI*
Women			
U.S. average (2002)	5'-3.8''	163 lbs.	28.2
Canada average (2005)	5'-3.4''	153 lbs.	26.8
Fashion model average	5'-10'' ±	118 lbs. ±	16.9
Men			
U.S. average (2002)	5'-9.3''	190 lbs.	27.8
Canada average (2005)	5'-8.5''	182 lbs.	27.3
Fashion model average	6'-0'' ±	178 lbs. ±	24.1

*BMI = Body Mass Index (Weight[kg] ÷ (Height[m] × Height[m])

Sources: U.S. National Center for Health Statistics
and Canadian Community Health Survey

Model proportions

There are several categories of modeling in the fashion industry. Height and size requirements are strict within each category because most clothing worn by models are pre-production samples made in only one size.

Fashion/editorial models (magazines, advertisements, catalog, and runway): Women are 5'-9" or taller, ideally with measurements of 34-24-34 (Size 4). Men range from 5'-11" to 6'-2", suit size 39 to 42 with 32" waist.

48

Showroom models: Used when retail stores visit manufacturers and design houses to try out styles for the upcoming season. Same sizes and measurements as fashion/editorial models.

Fit models: Used by design houses when creating production samples. For women, typically a Size 8; for men, Size 40R. The model must maintain ideal size for at least two months until production fitting is completed.

Plus-size (women) and big & tall (men) models: found in most or all modeling categories. Typically a Size 14 for women, Size XL/36" waist for men.

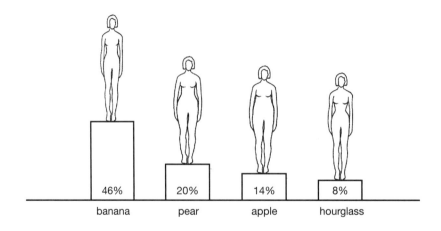

| 46% | 20% | 14% | 8% |
| banana | pear | apple | hourglass |

Women's body types by frequency
Source: North Carolina State University, 2005

If a garment looks good only on a six-foot-tall, 120-pound model, its designer hasn't done a good job.

49

The customers for a given collection may share similarities in how they live, think, and shop, but they aren't physically homogenous. A good collection offers a variety of silhouettes, proportions, and fabrics to suit a broad range of body types.

Petites
generally women
under 5'-4". Even
sizes, accompa-
nied by a P.

Juniors
usually younger
women who are
slim in the hips
and bust. Odd
sizes, typically 1
to 13.

Misses
women of aver-
age height and
proportion.
Even numbered
sizes, typically 0
to 14.

Plus sizes
large women,
designated by a
W, such as 14W
to 24W. Some
junior collections
are available in
plus sizes.

Grading

Designers typically work in women's Size 8 when designing for the middle market, and in Size 4 for the designer market. By *grading*—manipulating key measurements of the standard working size, including neckline to waist, shoulder to waist, cross-chest, front/back bustline, waist, bicep, and several others—other garments sizes may be created. Each design company uses an in-house grading formula, determined by the production manager, to guard proportional and styling consistency.

Plus and petite sizes require fundamental proportional adjustments to suit their wearers, and thus are not graded up or down from a Size 4 or 8 but are patterned and even designed separately. This is why collections in misses are often unavailable in plus and petite sizes.

50

Fabric selection is inseparable from color selection.

Designers envision color and fabric concurrently. White, for example, is not a meaningful design option until it is associated with a fabric: consider the great difference between crisp white linen and its creamy counterpart in wool, or the sophistication of hot pink in high fashion peau de soie (a soft, delustered silk) compared to its potentially vulgar counterpart in nylon or spandex.

51

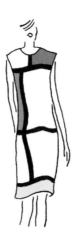

Mondrian dress by Yves St. Laurent

Primary colors have a limited audience.

Only a few garments are ever created in straight primary (yellow, red, or blue) or secondary (orange, purple, or green) colors. While a single garment in a basic color can be a great individual item, an entire collection in basic colors will have a quite limited audience. There are only a few times in a season that a customer will wear, for example, a bright yellow dress; but the same customer may wear the same dress in black, gray, or navy frequently.

Effective color palettes for a collection are usually families of color encountered in the world: for example, cosmetic colors, active colors, powder colors, sorbet colors, mineral colors, and earth, jewel, and spice tones.

52

Black and white aren't simply black and white.

All-black and all-white palettes might seem easy, but their uniformity demands that greater attention be given to more subtle considerations of texture, drape, and hand (the tactile feel of a fabric). Further, all blacks do not match: Warm blacks (those with a brownish undertone) and cool blacks (bluish undertone) can look shabby and inexpensive when combined.

All-white palettes can be similarly challenging. Summer whites may show off a suntan and creamy winter whites can be cozy and comforting. But cultural associations—with purity in the West and death in the East, for example—sometimes turn white into an awkward fashion choice. And like blacks, all whites don't automatically go together: Warm and cool whites can look dirty when combined.

53

Two views on fashion ambition

Make BIG mistakes. Avoid the path of least resistance. Set your goals and aspirations beyond your capabilities; it's better to aim for genius and miss than aim for mediocrity and hit it. Provoke reactions. Make design moves that are overly effusive just to see what happens. Don't do what you are already good at; try unfamiliar things to build a repertoire. Design too many garments and accessories for a collection, and scale back if necessary.

54

Minimize big moves. Keep big gestures to small doses. Avoid making every item in a collection a structurally or thematically complex showstopper; they will seem redundant, over-designed, and even dull. Just as in the theater, where background characters serve to make a feature character more remarkable, or in the symphony where a quiet interlude separates crescendos, an aggressive fashion move should be the exception among the more familiar.

Two ways to disappoint a design instructor

Do exactly what the instructor says. This tells the instructor, "I don't want to think." But an instructor's design suggestions aren't intended as the correct alternatives, but as a few avenues among many that you should explore to improve your project. In fact, the instructor might not at all be telling you what to do, but may be trying to steer you away from what not to do, from a design path that is unlikely to work out. Use an instructor's suggestions to catalyze your own creative responses.

Don't do what the instructor says. This tells the instructor, "I don't want to learn," that you think you know more than her, that you think she wants to take over the design of your collection, or that you think creativity suffers from criticism. In truth, your instructor is trying to lend insight into a design process with which she is more experienced than you. Trying out alternatives one is initially resistant to is an important component of good process.

55

Evolution of a design concept

Four design myths

Myth: Being creative means designing something that's never been seen before.
Reality: If something hasn't been seen before, it's probably not because it hasn't been thought of, but because it didn't work at the time.

Myth: Shopping for ideas is copying.
Reality: Idea shopping is a good designer's tool that enlarges one's mental repertoire of details, finishes, treatments, and more.

56

Myth: A successful final design looks like the original sketch.
Reality: A successful design concept evolves throughout the design process to best meet the customer's needs.

Myth: Reality equals banality.
Reality: Although fashion must have an aspirational, emotional, or even fantastical element, successful fashion designers dress real people.

Michelangelo was doing a job.

When Pope Julius II commissioned the painting of the Sistine Chapel ceiling, Michelangelo no doubt looked at the large surface broken up by many vaults, pendentives, and pilasters and feared the innumerable restrictions, boundaries, and boxes. He probably felt further limited by the demands of making the Bible understandable to a largely illiterate congregation.

It is unlikely, however, that Michelangelo complained he didn't like the ceiling, that it wasn't his style, or that the Pope didn't "get" how he worked. Instead, Michelangelo turned the practical limitations into artistic opportunities, lending testament to the true nature of creativity: It best reveals itself in solving real-world problems.

57

If you feel like a misunderstood genius, it might be because you're *not* a genius.

Even if you are a genius, the fault for being misunderstood is yours, as is the responsibility for becoming understood: You need to get better at communicating your ideas to the world.

It's not always a matter of taste.

Differences of opinion are common in fashion, but that doesn't mean all opinions are equal or the product of taste preferences. Perhaps more often they are due to differences in knowledge. Indeed, the greater one's knowledge of fabric, fit, structure, color, and tailoring, the more qualified his or her fashion opinion is.

Before dismissing the contrary opinion of a critic as a matter of personal preference, ask yourself, "Who between us would be more qualified as an expert in a court of law?" And consider the possibility that in embracing, rather than rejecting, the perspective of a critic, you will grow beyond your and your critic's current knowledge.

Shoe hat by Elsa Schiaparelli

"[Coco] Chanel has very little taste, all of it good. [Elsa] Schiaparelli has lots of taste, all of it bad."

—CRISTÓBAL BALENCIAGA

"A little bad taste is like a nice splash of paprika. We all need a splash of bad taste—it's hearty, it's healthy, it's physical. No taste is what I'm against."

—DIANA VREELAND

After a photograph by Alan Lindsay Gordon

Select fabrics by *hand*.

Color, texture, and pattern are crucial considerations in selecting fabric, but are nonetheless secondary to weight, character, and "hand"—a fabric's tactile feel. When browsing fabrics, try closing your eyes to prompt clearer judgments about hand quality.

62

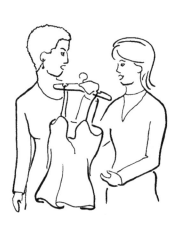

Remember hanger appeal.

Garments that are shoulderless or have spaghetti straps or wide neck openings can be difficult to display effectively in the retail environment. An otherwise well-designed garment may look unimpressive—or worse, like a rag—on a hanger, particularly with other appealing garments nearby. Not only may customers be unwilling to try it on; there's a good chance the store buyer won't give her a chance to do so.

Hanger loops are a simple fix for displaying a garment that won't stay on a hanger. However, overreliance on this solution may suggest a designer is ignoring the customer's needs: If more than perhaps five percent of a collection has this problem, the designer may be asking the customer to relentlessly exhibit too much skin.

After a painting by Mary Cassatt

Center back zippers are like fine crystal: best reserved for special occasions.

When a student designs an interesting garment and is asked how the wearer gets into it, the common answer is, "center back zipper." This solution is favored by inexperienced designers because it doesn't require an invasive change to a garment. But a back closure is rarely a satisfactory solution; it's a fussy, frustrating concern when one has only fifteen minutes to dress for work.

Back closures are a remnant from an era when women wore corsets and hoop-skirts and had maids to truss them up in back. Today, they are more appropriate in association with major events. On her wedding day or Oscar night, after a woman has spent a lot of time and money on her hair and makeup, she is more likely to want to step into her dress than pull it over her head. A center back zipper implies a fitting sense of occasion.

64

Chrysler PT Cruiser

There's a dangerous gray area between fashion and costume.

Traditionally, fashion has served to enhance a person's real persona, while costume has served to transform the wearer to a persona different from his or her natural one. When a fashion garment seems to be attempting the latter transformation, critics will often dismiss it as "too costumey."

In recent years, with influence from postmodern theory, it has become more popular to posit that there is no real self, only facades and projections. *All* is costume, says this view, even the most conventional garb. But a dangerous gray area remains, and designers and fashion wearers who enter it should be fully aware of the risks, resistances, and embarrassments that may be encountered.

You can't always play it straight.

Since the 1980s, irony has been the language of progressive fashion while conservative or traditional fashion has continued to "play it straight." John Bartlett's lumberjacks, for example, are intended as a cheeky, ironic reference to a homoerotic fantasy; he is not suggesting that his clients are or should become lumberjacks. But when Ralph Lauren shows aviators, huntsmen, and polo players on the fashion runway, he is literally suggesting a lifestyle to which his customers should or do aspire.

Generally, the more mature the customer, the more conservative, classic, and literal clothing should be. And when designing for the young, progressive customer, beware being overly literal, which may—ironically!—cross the line into costume.

When designing children's clothing, the parent is your customer.

Design clothes for infants, toddlers, and children under five years old with an eye toward their parents as the customer. The changing of diapers, cleanup of spills, and frequent washings—not to mention cost, as children can quickly ruin or outgrow clothes in a matter of months—can often overwhelm other design considerations.

67

Make children's clothing safe!

Hazards include:
- Drawstrings and cords that can cause strangulation or entrapment in a vehicle.
- Toggles, cord stops, and other hardware and trim that can cause choking.
- Lead and other toxins in hardware.
- Flammable fabrics.

68

Young customers have big heads.

In fashion illustration, a younger customer is usually suggested by a larger head, slender body, long hair, and soft pink or peach lips and cheeks. Curvy figures, short hair, graphic makeup (dark red lips, articulated lashes, and the like), and extra accessories (bracelets, necklaces) tend to suggest a more mature customer.

69

A fashion illustration should showcase the fashion, not the illustrator.

Talented illustrators naturally want to indulge and show off. But a good artist is a self-editor who checks such impulses. He or she constantly revisits the question, "What is the minimum that will effectively communicate the design?"

70

Illustration don'ts

Don't be creative with light. The light source should be located at the top left or right, with figures facing it in profile or ¾ view. Figures looking away from the light source will tend to have distracting shadows on their faces. Shadows should fall under the chin, bust, and hem, and behind the arm or leg farthest from the viewer.

Don't overdo shadows. A rendering of drapery by an old master may have been beautifully modeled with heavy shadows, but a fashion rendering should be schematic and editorial.

Don't overarticulate. A fashion sketch should communicate a customer, not an actual person. Develop a repertoire of minimalist faces you can use all the time.

Don't overuse lines. Too many lines can lend a coloring book quality to a sketch. Use lines sparingly to emphasize details.

71

Don't be careless with proportions. Many illustrations of a garment or collection can be in use in a design studio or office at one time. Patternmakers and drapers may use croquis and flats as working guides, embroiderers may use blow-ups to determine placement, and a production manager might use sketches for estimating costs. In each illustration, consistency of part to part and part to whole must be maintained.

¾ side pose

What pose best shows it?

When deciding on a pose, consider the silhouette and details that must be communicated. The wrong pose can misrepresent a design and mislead the intended customer.

Figure in standing repose: Use to show off slim skirts and dressy styles. For layered ensembles, a hand on the hip reveals underpinnings. Not best for flowing garments, which can appear wooden and heavy on a static figure.

Dynamic/walking figure: Use for flowing fabrics, garments with full silhouettes, and active or casual sport looks. Be careful with slim outfits; a pencil skirt on a figure with splayed legs may inadvertently suggest an A-line skirt.

72

Figure in profile: Most effective in showing off a dramatic silhouette, such as a full swing jacket over a pencil skirt, and for displaying special side detailing.

Back (rear) figures: Use only for showing important back details.

Michelangelo's *David*

Low shoulder, high hip

Before drawing a figure, first draw the head, then a vertical plumb line down the page, and then the intended location of the feet. The desired weight distribution of the figure determines the location of the feet relative to the plumb line. If evenly distributed (static figure), the feet are spaced equally on both sides. If the weight is entirely on one leg, that leg and foot will be exactly on the plumb line, with the other leg and foot off to the side. If both feet are on the same side of the plumb line, the figure will appear to be falling.

In *contrapposto*, a figure is rendered with all weight on one foot and the shoulders and arms twisted slightly off-axis from the hips and legs. The side of the body with the lower shoulder will have the higher hip.

73

Skin is translucent.

Skin is not opaque; it allows light to pass through. This is why your hand appears red when you hold it up to the sun. When illustrating the human figure, allowing some of the white of the page to show through will keep your figures from looking lifeless, doll-like, or cartoonish.

Watercolor, gouache, and tempera are the most effective media for rendering flesh convincingly. Design markers are good for translucency, but are of limited value because they have to be the exact desired color.

Pastels and color pencils are not often used in fashion illustration, as they emphasize the grain of the paper and the hand of the illustrator. Acrylics and oil paints are of limited or no value because they do not allow translucency.

74

Avoid the firing line.

When drawing multiple figures, an apparent solution is to align them in a row. But for a collection having similar color or silhouette throughout, the result can be dull repetitiveness. And a collection with a *lot* of variety may appear incoherent.

   Make compositions containing multiple figures *dynamic*. Make arrangements asymmetrical, with background figures higher on the page than those in front. Overlap figures slightly, making sure not to obscure shapes or important design details. Group figures in twos and threes, and make them aware of each other.

75

Counterpoint clothing with hair and skin color.

For best effect in illustration try pairing:
- darker clothes with fair skin and light clothes with darker skin.
- a green fashion palette with red or reddish-brown hair.
- a red fashion palette with black or blonde hair.
- a yellow fashion palette with black, brown, or red hair.
- a blue fashion palette with any color hair. However, dark hair will lend elegance and sophistication to baby blue, while blonde hair will soften the potential severity of navy blue by suggesting girlishness.

Step back and take a look.

When creating a garment or sketch, one necessarily works at arm's length or closer. But good designers and illustrators take continual steps back to see how their creations look from the distances at which they are likely to be viewed by others. Designers who view their work only from working distance are invariably disappointed on presentation day, when their work turns out to look very different from expectation.

77

Render patterns generally, not literally.

When rendering a print or woven pattern, don't show every petal of every flower or every check in a houndstooth. Instead, envision what the pattern would look like if seen on an actual model standing far enough away to appear the same size as your drawing (typically 12 to 14 inches tall). You might find that tiny multicolored prints or micro-patterns merge into an overall color, and middle-scale patterns read as a texture.

78

Good fashion is like freestanding sculpture: interesting from every angle.

Novice designers often focus their efforts on the front of a garment, treating the back and sides as leftovers holding everything together. But this rarely results in a satisfactory garment.

When croquis-ing or sketching, try inverting your process: First apply your design concept to the *back* of the garment, and design from there. Often you will find that the center back zipper impulse proves immediately unsatisfying, and a center front zipper unwieldy. New ideas for both the back and front will emerge and an overall more satisfying design will result.

Similarly, by applying the design concept to the sides, new opportunities may be realized. A creative side seam might be understood as a visual transition that helps the front "reveal" the back. Or creative stitching and fabric placement opportunities may be discovered to complement the front or back of the garment.

79

"Art produces ugly things which frequently become beautiful with time. Fashion, on the other hand, produces beautiful things which always become ugly with time."

—JEAN COCTEAU

80

Florence Griffith Joyner, track star
(1959–1998)

Asymmetry implies nudity.

Symmetrical garments are far more common than asymmetrical ones because of the symmetry of the human body. But asymmetry can be beautiful and provocative, at least in part because it suggests dressing and undressing. A symmetrical display of skin feels deliberate, secure, and final, but a bare shoulder or arm can suggest that something has fallen off—and something else may yet come off!

81

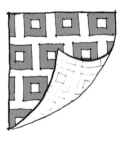

Printed

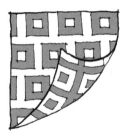

Yarn-died

Visual patterns

Yarn-dyed patterns are woven or knitted into a fabric during manufacture using different color yarns. The pattern shows on both the face and reverse. Plaid, check, stripe, floral, mottled, and abstract geometric patterns are common examples.

Printed patterns are applied to an already woven or knitted fabric using various dye and ink processes including flatbed, rotary, transfer, discharge, and silk-screening. A printed pattern is typically visible on the face of a fabric but only partially or not at all visible on the reverse.

Patterns that are typically produced as woven patterns, for example pinstripes and checks, can look low end when printed. On the other hand, a finely detailed floral print may use ten or more colors, producing an exquisite pattern that would be virtually impossible to create in a yarn-dyed fabric.

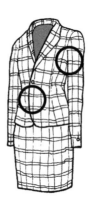

There's no perfect match.

When designing with visual patterns, matches have to be compromised at some seams to achieve matches in more critical areas. Give primary consideration to:

Sleeve-body matching: The pattern on the bicep (one or two inches below the armhole) should match the pattern directly across on the bustline or chest.

Center seam matching: Because of the body's contours, vertical lines unavoidably undulate. When working with plaids and vertical stripes, maintaining symmetry around the center seam will lend a sense of deliberateness to pattern placement. If the pattern is multi-color, it is usually best to place a less prominent vertical stripe at the center seam.

On highly randomized print patterns such as florals, it can be cost prohibitive and even impossible to achieve consistent seam matches. Some high-end designers will place a single prominent element, such as a large flower or medallion, so that it is matched up on a prominent seam such as the center-front chest.

Usually not successful:
- small patterns with other small patterns
- big patterns with other big patterns
- same patterns together, e.g., checks with other checks, stripes with stripes, etc.

Usually successful:
- small patterns with large patterns
- counterpointed patterns, e.g., geometrics with swirls, regularized with randomized, segmented with continuous, etc.

Combining visual patterns

The most effective tool for the harmonious mixing of visual patterns is *counterpoint*. **Scale counterpoint** means grouping patterns of dissimilar scales, i.e., a larger pattern with a smaller pattern. A failure to counterpoint scale will result in either visual cacophony (two large patterns together) or the "measles" (two small patterns together).

Type counterpoint means placing stripes with curves, regularized with randomized, florals with windowpanes, etc., rather than stripes with stripes, florals with florals, and so on. If similar patterns are used together, their scales need to be very different. For example, two floral patterns might be pairable if one is very small scale and the other very large; or two striped patterns can be placed together if one is a close-spaced pinstripe and the other a wide rep stripe.

The more perfectly matched a fabric group, the lower-end it tends to look.

A preoccupation with perfect matching—that jacket and skirt or belt and shoes must match exactly, or that tie and pocket square should be in identical patterns—betrays a mechanical, one-to-one sensibility that is not that of the aesthetic-minded person. Designers of refined taste have nuanced understandings of color and pattern relationships; they can hit the right notes with nonchalance and eclecticism rather than literalism.

85

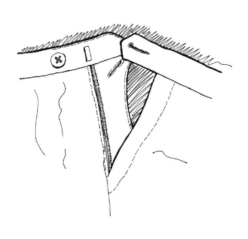

When in doubt, look in your closet.

When unsure about how a garment you've designed should be constructed, look at your own wardrobe: We all have at least one pair of fly-front pants and a garment that buttons down the front. It doesn't take much time or effort to pull it out and replicate or adapt what one sees.

86

The mirror is your best friend.

A true friend, perhaps unlike a colleague or classmate, is always honest and forthright, with no agendas or ulterior motives. Looking at one's work in a mirror is like finding a new best friend: You probably will notice something you didn't see before. A figure you thought was standing firmly on the page might appear to be falling over. A flat you thought perfectly symmetrical is uneven; a muslin you believed beautifully draped is puckering and pulling; or a neckline you thought flattering turns out to make the bustline look too low.

A good fit model tells a designer what does and doesn't work.

A sample or muslin fitting involves many people: designers, patternmakers, sample-makers, assistants, and a model. Because of the intensity of the effort and the need to work fluidly as a team, verbal and non-verbal shorthand are required.

A good fit model is part of the communication process. He or she understands what is needed without being asked. A hand on the hip or shoulder may mean "turn this way," while a hand on the wrist says, "lift your arm." Additionally, a good fit model will tell the designer what doesn't feel right, and may even be able to tell a designer the exact cause of a problem and how to fix it.

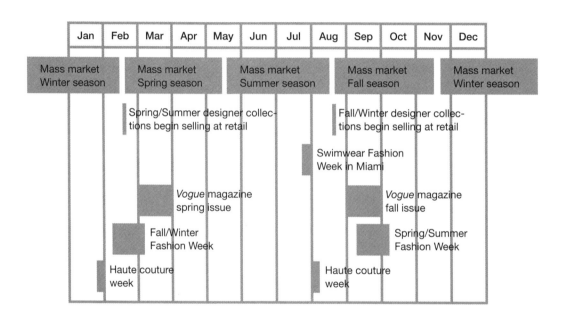

88

The upper end of the fashion industry uses a 2-season annual calendar. The lower end uses a 4-season calendar.

Designers show their seasonal collections twice each year during Fashion Week, the major event of the fashion industry. Fashion Week actually lasts four weeks, during which fashion buyers and editors from around the world travel in sequence to New York, London, Milan, and Paris to preview the upcoming season at hundreds of runway shows. Afterward, they visit the showrooms of fashion designers to make their seasonal selections or schedule photo shoots for fashion magazines.

The lower end of the industry, which consists of mass market, moderate, and lifestyle brands, divides the year into four seasons and twelve deliveries. Three months are allotted to each season, and new products are delivered to stores every month. The seasons are called Spring I, Spring II or Summer, Fall, and Holiday. Children's and Junior markets sometimes use "Back-to-School" to indicate the Fall season.

89

Displaying the goods

Grocery store method: In large department stores, similar merchandise is commonly displayed together. The retail floor is roughly divided into separate areas individually containing suits, dresses, jeans, and so on.

Boutique method: Each designer has a boutique within a larger store. A boutique contains the store's purchase of the designer's seasonal collection.

Cross merchandising: This is the display of diverse products (shirts, shoes, accessories, etc.) in one thematic setting, perhaps according to color or trend. This can increase the perceived value of secondary items (e.g., underpinnings such as camis or tanks, or accessories such as scarves or bags) that might otherwise be overlooked by the shopper by directing attention to the full complement of products needed for a particular fashion look. This method is often used by small stores where floor space is at a premium, and is used increasingly in large retailers in combination with other display methods.

Sportswear isn't clothing worn for sports.

Sportswear is factory-made, off-the-rack coordinated separates sold in standard sizes. It may include daywear, career, day-to-night, cocktail, casual, and evening clothes. Sportswear is the American equivalent of what the French call *Prêt-à-Porter*, or Ready-to-Wear. Clothing worn for sports is called *active wear*.

91

Jeans = sex.

Blue jeans originally were equated with work: They were used by miners, prospectors, and laborers. Today the rivets, bar-tacks, and saddle-stitching intended for rough wear have become design features connoting "authenticity." That jeans will show wear while remaining useful for many years is part of this authenticity: Evidence of wear is often designed into them before they are ever worn.

The feature of jeans that enabled them to enter the realm of fashion is a unique center seam. It hugs the curves of the behind, and in men projects the crotch forward from where it would be in a conventional trouser. Without this "must-do" feature, all the rivets, stitching, and sandblasting in the world will not make a proper pair of jeans.

Don't hassle me
with your rules,
man.

I'm business on
top, and fun on
the bottom.

No, I can't see,
but they make
you see me.

I'm on the
move.

Fashion is *commentary*.

Fashion is not simply nice clothing; it provides relevant commentary—on the wearer, on what others are wearing, on fashions that have come and gone, on the human body, and on the culture. This is partly why fashions are ephemeral; once the commentary provided by a fashion becomes familiar and generally understood, the dialogue moves on. It is also why, when a style is "recycled," something about it is different: The miniskirt is flounced, the trumpet skirt is paired with flats instead of heels, the narrow lapel jacket is worn with a primary color instead of white shirt. The conversation has returned to a familiar topic, but with new things to say.

Fashion-as-commentary means it is possible to be well dressed without being fashionable, or even poorly dressed—by the standards of some, at least—but very fashionable.

T-shirt by Katharine Hamnett

"The primitive man in the wolf pelt was not keeping dry; he was saying, 'Look what I killed. Aren't I the best?'"

—KATHARINE HAMNETT

94

In leather, emphasize the details.

Leather, because it is the skin of an animal, doesn't come in continuous yardage. Consequently, a leather garment usually has more seams than an equivalent garments in fabric. Further, the finer the leather, the smaller the pieces tend to be.

Because piecing and seams are so crucial—and because leather shows off stitching beautifully—leather garments are frequently designed in a way that emphasizes and celebrates their details.

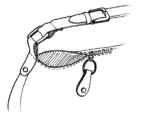

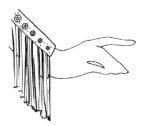

Hardware, including buttons, zippers, snaps, toggles, rivets and grommets, are essential to the function of a garment.

Embellishments, including embroidery, beading, and trims, are purely decorative.

Hardware and embellishments should further, and not simply accompany, a design concept.

Napoleon Bonaparte
(1769–1821)

Why men and women button on opposite sides

Two theories have currency: One is that men of a different era had to be prepared to retrieve a sword or pistol from inside their clothing at a moment's notice. A left-side-over-right-side orientation allowed the easiest access for the right-handed.

Another theory is that "proper" ladies were once dressed by their maids; a right-side-over-left-side buttoning best accommodated a right-handed maid.

A good designer doesn't rely on styling.

Fashion design is the skillful arrangement of aesthetic and structural elements to create garments and collections. **Styling** is the arrangement of garments and accessories on a model, mannequin, or display to project a specific look, persona, or attitude.

A stylist doesn't have to be able to design, but a designer does need to understand styling. Frequent sketches of complete head-to-toe looks including all accessories—hats, hair, makeup, jewelry, facial hair, shoes, boots, socks, belts, gloves, etc.—will help a designer maintain a sense of proportion among the parts and of parts to whole. Often, each will inform the other; not to mention that a break from focusing on clothes will often help free up a designer's creative process.

Don't rely on styling to pull off a fashion design, however. If you find that you strongly intend specific accessories to go with a garment you are designing, there is a good chance it is because their aesthetic sensibility wants to be directly incorporated into the garment.

98

A successful professional thinks big *and* small.

A fashion designer must be able to conceive an entire clothing collection twelve months in advance of a fashion season. This requires an ability to holistically assess broad cultural developments, fashion trends, evolving customer needs, budgets, and the processes required for manufacture and delivery. At the same time, a designer has to realize every item in a collection in minute detail—from its proportions and fabric to the specific color of thread and size of buttons.

99

Johnny Cash
(1932–2003)

True style is innate.

What we recognize as visual style is the surface revelation of something existing at a deeper level. Style is not simply how things look; it's how they are. A genuinely stylish person is not one who has learned to look a certain way, but one who *is* a certain way—a way that has expression in visual form.

100

"Fashions fade, style is eternal."

—YVES ST. LAURENT

Alfredo Cabrera is a fashion designer, teacher, and illustrator who has taught, lectured, and served as critic at Parsons The New School for Design, Fashion Institute of Technology, Pratt Institute, and the Altos de Chavón School of Design. He lives in New York City.

Matthew Frederick is an architect, urban designer, teacher, author of the bestselling *101 Things I Learned in Architecture School*, and the creator, editor, and illustrator of the 101 Things I Learned series. He lives in Cambridge, Massachusetts.